The Life and Work of...

Michelángelo Buonarroti

Richard Tames

Heinemann
LIBRARY

www.heinemann.co.uk
Visit our website to find out more information about Heinemann Library books.

To order:
 Phone 44 (0) 1865 888066
 Send a fax to 44 (0) 1865 314091
 Visit the Heinemann Bookshop at www.heinemann.co.uk to browse our catalogue and order online.

First published in Great Britain by Heinemann Library,
Halley Court, Jordan Hill, Oxford OX2 8EJ
a division of Reed Educational and Professional
Publishing Ltd.
Heinemann is a registered trademark of Reed
Educational & Professional Publishing Ltd.

OXFORD MELBOURNE AUCKLAND
JOHANNESBURG BLANTYRE GABORONE
IBADAN PORTSMOUTH (NH) USA CHICAGO

Designed by Celia Floyd
Illustrations by Sam Thompson
Originated by Dot Gradations
Printed in Hong Kong/China

ISBN 0 431 09196 X (hardback)
05 04 03 02 01
10 9 8 7 6 5 4 3 2 1

ISBN 0 431 09201 X (paperback)
05 04 03 02 01
10 9 8 7 6 5 4 3 2 1

British Library Cataloguing in Publication Data

Tames, Richard, 1946–
    Life and work of Michelangelo Buonarroti
    1. Michelangelo – Juvenile literature
    2. Painters – Italy – Biography – Juvenile literature
    3. Painting, Renaissance – Italy – Juvenile literature
    4. Painting, Italian – Juvenile literature
    I. Title
    II. Michelangelo Buonarroti
    759.5

Acknowledgements
The Publishers would like to thank the following for
permission to reproduce photographs:

Archivi Alinari: pp5, 9, 11, 13, 15, 21; Archivio
Buonarroti: p27; Bridgeman Art Library: Casa
Buonarroti, Florence p7, Vatican Museums and Galleries,
Italy p17; E T Archive: p28; J Allan Cash Ltd: p23; Photo
RMN: R G Ojeda p19; Robert Harding Picture Library:
Simon Harris p25; Scala, Museo delli Opera del Duomo:
p29

Cover photograph reproduced with permission of The
Bridgeman Art Library

Every effort has been made to contact copyright holders
of any material reproduced in this book. Any omissions
will be rectified in subsequent printings if notice is given
to the Publisher.

Any words appearing in the text in bold, **like this**, are
explained in the Glossary.

Contents

Who was Michelangelo?   4

The pupil   6

The student   8

Fame   10

Working in Florence   12

The Pope's tomb   14

The Sistine Chapel   16

Cities at war   18

Working for the Medici   20

Back to Rome   22

The Pope's architect   24

Last years   26

Michelangelo dies   28

Timeline   30

Glossary   31

More books to read and more art to see   31

Index   32

Who was Michelangelo?

Michelangelo was one of the greatest artists of the Italian **Renaissance**. He thought of himself as a **sculptor**, but he was also a painter, a poet and an **architect**.

Michelangelo's painting of God giving life to Adam is on the ceiling of the Sistine **Chapel** in Rome, Italy. In Michelangelo's time most art was made for churches.

The pupil

Michelangelo was born on 6 March 1475 in Caprese, Italy. His family moved to Florence a few weeks after he was born. At school he wanted to become a painter. The rich Medici family let him study the works of art they owned.

Soon, however, Michelangelo became interested in **sculpture** as well. He was only 16 when he carved this sculpture of the baby Jesus with his mother, Mary.

The student

Michelangelo longed to understand how the human body worked. So he studied human bodies in a hospital in Florence. This helped him make his paintings and **sculptures** look real.

Michelangelo also studied the work of other artists. He made his own drawings of **frescoes**, like this one, by the Italian artist Masaccio. This taught him about the use of colour and **perspective**.

9

Fame

Michelangelo moved to Rome in 1496. He carved a **statue** of Jesus lying dead in Mary's arms. This statue made him famous.

The statue was for a church. It is called the *Pietà*.
Michelangelo made the two very different figures
– one a man and one a woman, one dead and
one alive – from a single piece of stone.

Working in Florence

In 1501 Michelangelo returned to Florence. He had been asked to make a **statue** of **David** for the city's **cathedral**.

Michelangelo's statue of David became famous. People thought it showed what a perfect human being would look like.

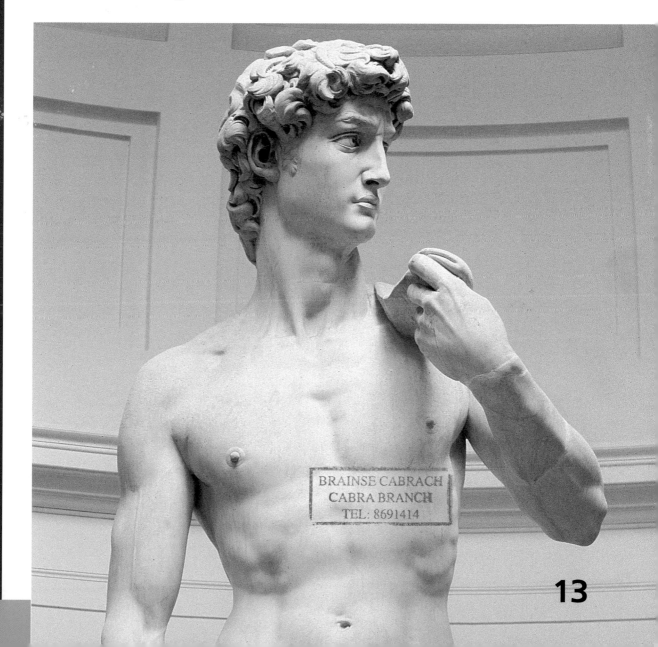

The Pope's tomb

In 1505 Michelangelo planned a huge **tomb** for **Pope** Julius II, in Rome. But Michelangelo often took on more work than he had time to do, and the tomb was never finished.

The tomb was to have had over 40 **statues** on it. This one of **Moses** was meant to go in the middle. Moses looks very real – even down to his sandals.

The Sistine Chapel

In 1508 **Pope** Julius II asked Michelangelo to paint the ceiling of the Sistine **Chapel** in Rome. Michelangelo didn't really want to do it, because he liked working on **sculptures** better.

It took Michelangelo four years to paint the ceiling. The paintings tell stories from the Bible. They are among the most famous paintings in the world.

Cities at war

Italy was often at war during Michelangelo's lifetime. Between 1528 and 1529 he worked on plans for buildings and walls to protect Florence during an attack.

Michelangelo made this sketch in 1528. It shows his plans for the defence of Florence. He wanted ditches to be made all round the city.

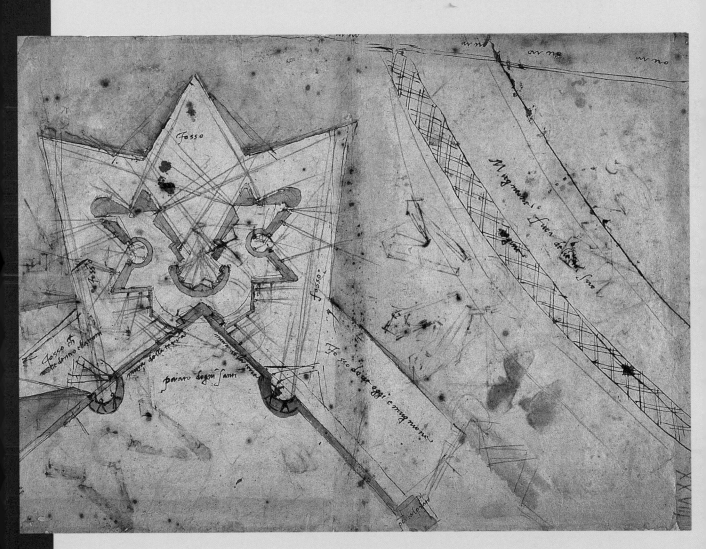

Working for the Medici

From 1515 until 1534 Michelangelo worked for the Medici family in Florence. He **designed** a **chapel**, a library, two **tombs** and a grand house for them.

This is one of the tombs Michelangelo designed for the Medici family. The two figures at the front are meant to be Dawn and Dusk.

Back to Rome

From 1534 until he died, Michelangelo lived in Rome. He **designed** a new square for the centre of the city.

Michelangelo redesigned the old city hall on Capitolene Hill. He also produced a special floor design of oval patterns with a **statue** at the centre.

The Pope's architect

In 1546 Michelangelo became the **Pope**'s main **architect**. He worked on the great church of St Peter in Rome.

Michelangelo **designed** the **dome** of St Peter's.
Sadly he died before he saw it finished.

Last years

In 1546 to 1547 Michelangelo **designed** a palace for **Pope** Paul III's family to live in. He also wrote many poems and letters to his friends and family.

Michelangelo was left-handed and he had beautiful handwriting. Many of his poems are about love, even though he never got married.

Michelangelo dies

Michelangelo died on 18 February 1564. He was 88 years old. He was buried in Florence in a **tomb designed** by a pupil of his called Giorgio Vasari. Giorgio also wrote a **biography** of Michelangelo.

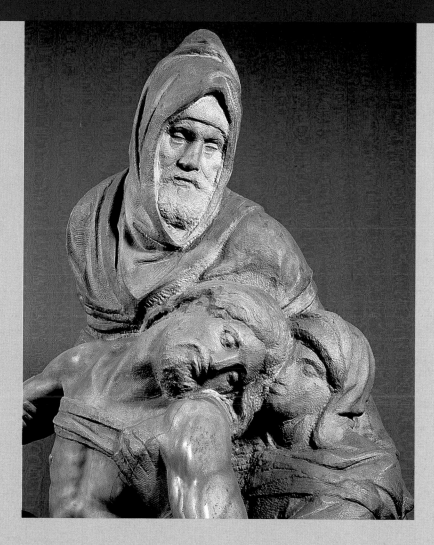

This is part of a **statue** Michelangelo was making
for his own tomb, but he never finished it.
It shows Michelangelo himself, at 75 years old.

Timeline

1475 — Michelangelo Buonarroti born in Caprese, Italy on 6 March.

1483 — The artist Raphael was born.

1488 — Michelangelo is trained by the artist Ghirlandaio.

1490–1492 — Michelangelo lives in the Medici Palace.

1496 — Michelangelo moves from Florence to Rome.

1501–1504 — Michelangelo carves **statue** of **David**.

1508–1512 — Michelangelo paints ceiling of Sistine **Chapel**.

1513 — **Pope** Julius II dies.

1519 — The artist Leonardo da Vinci dies.

1520 — The artist Raphael dies.

1528–1529 — Michelangelo **designs** defences for Florence.

1534 — Michelangelo leaves Florence for the last time.

1534–1541 — Michelangelo paints **fresco** (*The Last Judgement*) for a wall in the Sistine Chapel.

1546 — Michelangelo becomes the Pope's chief **architect**.

1550 — Giorgio Vasari writes the first **biography** of Michelangelo.

1564 — Michelangelo dies on 18 February.

Glossary

architect person who designs buildings

biography story of a person's life

cathedral large and important church

chapel small church or part of a bigger church or cathedral

David hero of the Bible and later King of Israel

design to think of an idea or plan and put it on paper

dome rounded roof

fresco painting done on wet plaster so the colour soaks in

Moses Bible hero given the stones with the Ten Commandments by God

perspective way of drawing to show distance

Pope leader of the Roman Catholic Church

Renaissance time when artists copied the styles of ancient Greece and Rome

sculptor person who carves wood or stone to make works of art

sculpture statue or carving

statue carved, moulded or sculptured figure of a person or animal

tomb place to be buried in

More books to read

Famous Artists: Michelangelo, Franklin Watts

Leonardo da Vinci, Sean Connolly, Heinemann Library

More art to see

The Entombment, National Gallery, London

Tondo Taddei, Royal Academy of Arts, London

David (copy), Victoria and Albert Museum, London

Index

biography   28

birth   6

death   28

Medici family   6, 20, 21

Pope Julius II   14, 16, 19

Pope Paul III   24, 26

Sistine Chapel   5, 16, 17

St Peter's   24, 25

Statue of David   12, 13

war   18, 19